S0-BYM-992

SPEAK RIGHT UP

Public Speaking Training Program of

Young Speakers Club

SPEAK RIGHT UP

Public Speaking Training Program of

Young Speakers Club

RICE PUBLIC LIBRARY
8 WENTWORTH ST.
KITTERY, MAINE 03904
207-439-1553

Abe George

American Media House
Fairfax VA 22030

Speak Right Up
Public Speaking Training Program of Young Speakers Club

by **Abe George**

Published by American Media House
Fairfax, Virginia, U.S.A.
tel. 703 383 6649
www.AmericanMediaHouse.com

Young Speakers Club is a non-profit organization dedicated to the training of students interested in public speaking and leadership.

Website: www.YoungSpeakersClub.net
Email: YoungSpeakersClub@gmail.com

ISBN: 978-0-9776091-2-3

Copyright © 2008 by Abe George
All rights reserved.

Books may be purchased in bulk at special discounts for promotional or educational purposes. Special editions can be created to specifications. All inquiries should be addressed to: Abe George, 5042 Huntwood Manor Drive, Fairfax, VA, 22030.

10 9 8 7 6 5 4 3 2 1

Table of Contents

1

What is the Young Speakers Club Program?

Your decision to develop your public speaking skills, or to improve the skills you have, is one of the most important decisions in your life that will help you in your career, social life, and in your personal life. The program offered in this book will guide you in the right direction with which to develop and to improve your public speaking skills.

Good public speaking skills are necessary for excellence in many areas, including:

- ▶ Class Presentations;
- ▶ Team Leadership;
- ▶ Confidence Building; and
- ▶ Career Advancement.

This book draws from the vast wealth of experiences that I have gained in training students in the art of public speaking and leadership. As the founder and the president of the Young Speakers Club, a non-profit organization, I have diligently trained students over the years who aspire to enhance their public speaking and leadership skills.

The Young Speakers Club focuses on developing and improving the public speaking skills and stage comfort of students through a series of entertaining training sessions. Students are guided to develop and perform speeches, standup comedies, subject teachings, or report presentations. The classes are a combination of lessons, performances, and workshops, designed to teach the necessary skills for all types of stage performances, interactively.

Public speaking skills development is not a two-month or a two-year program; rather, it is an ongoing process. A training class for a fixed period can only provide general concepts and some initial training. I encourage each of you to find a group similar to the Young Speakers Club where you could further enhance your skills. If you would like to start a Young Speakers Club in your area, check the Web site www.YoungSpeakersClub.net for additional detailed information. You should also utilize every opportunity you can get to do stage performances, each of which will be giving you more and more stage comfort.

Notes:

_____

_____

_____

_____

_____

_____

_____

_____

_____

_____

_____

There are three things to aim at in public speaking; first to get into your subject, then to get your subject into yourself, and lastly, to get your subject into your hearers.

A.S. GREGG

What This Program Offers

The Young Speakers Club program is designed to provide its students lessons and training guidance for developing the fundamental skills that are necessary for effective public speaking. As public speaking is an essential quality for leadership, this program addresses effective leadership also, but only within the scope of public speaking.

Lessons and training sessions for public speaking skills development

- ▶ How do you develop a good speech?
- ▶ What are the essential components of a good speech?
- ▶ How do you research and craft a good speech?
- ▶ Why is eye contact very important?
- ▶ How do you practice eye contact?
- ▶ How to use your hand and body gestures to power your speech?
- ▶ How to use your whole body as a visual aid for your presentation?
- ▶ How to use voice modulation to make your speech more interesting and dramatic?
- ▶ How to form context sensitive and audience sensitive pitch and modulation?
- ▶ How to practice the speech?
- ▶ How can you display professionalism and confidence to your audiences?
- ▶ How can you handle emergencies?
- ▶ What to do and what not to do when things go wrong?

Lessons and training for leadership skills development

- ▶ How to manage a meeting?
- ▶ How to introduce a speaker?
- ▶ How to provide instructions to a group?

Notes:

_____

_____

_____

_____

_____

_____

_____

_____

_____

_____

_____

_____

On speaking, first have something to say, second say it, third stop when you have said it, and finally give it an accurate title.

JOHN SHƏW BILLINGS

How to Study This Program

This is an introductory course in public speaking. The lessons and techniques that you learn here are valid not just for public speaking, but also for any type of stage performances. Learn them properly now, as described in each of the lessons, and they will stay with you for a lifetime.

After studying each lesson, follow the exercises at the end, which require students to perform what they have learned in front of a group. At this point, it doesn't matter the number of people in the group; you can even start with just two or three people in your family. What matters is how you are performing what you have learned. Make sure that you always stand up in front of the group whenever you practice and perform.

You should repeat the performances many times, maybe for several months, to reinforce the public speaking skills in you. Once you are comfortable with a specific skill you have been developing, move on to the next lesson and start applying the skills in that lesson. By the time that you finish all of the lessons, your stage comfort will be significantly improved and you will know how to incorporate the fundamental skills of public speaking in all of your performances.

Initially, as you start applying each skill in your performances, it may appear to you and others as animated or artificial. Don't worry about it, because as you practice more and more, these skills will become natural to you. The key is to continue performing in front of different groups whenever you get the opportunity to do so, which is the only way that the public speaking skills can become natural to you.

The success of this program depends on the effort that you put into the program, practicing the lessons, and the number of times that you perform them in formal settings. It is important that even if you are presenting a speech or a standup comedy to a small group (just two or three people), you should present it with all of the seriousness of a formal meeting.

The Three P's of Public Speaking

PRACTICE *and*
PERFORM *to reach*
PERFECTION

Notes: _____

_____

_____

_____

_____

_____

_____

_____

_____

_____

_____

Happiness, wealth, and success are by-products of goal setting; they cannot be goal themselves.
DENIS WAITLEY

4

Types of public speaking

There are four major categories of public speaking and multiple sub-categories within each one. The reasons for public speaking can be defined within each category or sub-category. Listed below are some of the subcategories within each majaor category.

1. **Speeches to inspire the audiences:**
   ▶ Sermons – for the spiritual and personal improvements of the audiences
   ▶ Campaign speech – requesting audiences for action
   ▶ Keynote speeches – encouraging audiences

2. **Speeches to entertain the audiences:**
   ▶ Standup comedy – make people laugh
   ▶ Toasting – Congratulate
   ▶ Luncheon and dinner speeches – entertain the audiences

3. **Speeches to educate the audiences:**
   ▶ Teaching
   ▶ Technical presentations
   ▶ Seminar and conference presentations
   ▶ Office discussions
   ▶ Public policy speeches
   ▶ Debates and legal arguments

4. **Speeches to perform administrative responsibilities:**

    ▶ Master of ceremony

    ▶ Chair of the meeting or meeting administrator

    ▶ Host/hostess

Notes: _____

_____

_____

_____

_____

_____

_____

_____

_____

_____

_____

> Use what talent you have; the woods would have little music if no birds sang their songs except those who sang best
> **REVERAND OLIVER G WILSON**

Introducing a Speaker

When you have the responsibility to introduce a speaker, make sure that your introduction includes three important parts.

1. **Who is the speaker?**

   ► Name

   ► Credentials

   ► Why is he/she the right person to speak on the topic

2. **What is the topic?**

   ► Title of the speech

   ► Specific areas within the topic that will be addressed

3. **Why the specific topic is chosen?**

   ► The topic's importance to the audience

   ► The topic's importance to the organization/state/country

---

Example

Ladies and Gentlemen,

We are privileged to have President Abraham Lincoln as our speaker for this evening. As the U.S. president who helped preserve the United States by leading the defeat of the secessionist Confederate States in the Civil War and as the president who abolished slavery, he is considered as one of the most respected world leaders of all times. He witnessed and experienced the atrocities and struggles of war, not only on the soldiers, but also on the families of the soldiers and the citizens of the country as well. So, he is the ideal person to give a speech on the topic, "Stop the War" to the families of soldiers assembled here, who are now experiencing the struggles of a new war almost about 150 years after the civil war. Let's extend a warm welcome to President Abraham Lincoln.

EXERCISE

1. **Do self introduction:**

   ■ **What is the topic?**

   ■ **What are my credentials to speak about this topic?**

   ■ **What is the importance of this topic?**

2. **Introduce the person next to you:**

   ■ **Make sure that your introduction includes the three main parts discussed in the lesson.**

Notes: _____

_____

_____

_____

_____

_____

_____

_____

_____

_____

_____

Preparing a Speech

For the practice sessions, you should prepare speeches on topics that you are very comfortable with. The less memorization you have to do, the better. You should prepare the speeches in your own words, so that it will be easier for you to present it. Chapter 7 gives you a list of topics that you can either choose from for your speech or use as a guideline to develop a topic of your own. You can develop a speech or a comedy or a teaching session from these topics.

Once you have decided on the topic for your speech, you should do research to find materials to be included in the speech. There are several ways to research a topic, including the following:

▶ Talk to your family, teachers, and friends;

▶ Read magazine articles and newspaper articles on the topic;

▶ Read books on the topic;

▶ Refer to an encyclopedia; and

▶ Search on the Internet.

When preparing a speech using the information that you have collected through research, there are certain steps that you can take to make the work easier.

▶ Note down all of the points that you have collected and group them based on their nature. One such grouping that you can use is by asking questions, such as: WHAT, WHY, HOW, WHERE, WHO, WHEN, etc.

▶ Assign importance to each of the points by indicating whether it is a "must in clude in the speech" (MUST) point or "may include in the speech" (MAY) point.

▶ All speeches should consist of three parts: Introduction, Speech Body, and Con clusion.

▶ Prepare a catchy introduction and a memorable conclusion. The catchy intro duction will hook the audience to your speech, and the memorable conclusion will leave a lasting impression about your speech in their minds. Chapter 8 shows you an example of a catchy introduction and a memorable conclusion.

▶ Write the first draft of your speech and time it by reading it aloud.

▶ Refine the draft by trimming the fat and making the speech flow smoothly.

▶ Refine it further as you practice by introducing voice modulation techniques.

EXERCISE

1. **Refer chapter 7 for speech ideas and select one topic that interests you.**

2. **Study chapter 8 to understand how introductions and conclusions are crafted.**

3. **Using the guidelines given in this chapter, prepare a speech.**

4. **Perform your speech.**

Speech Ideas

Abraham Lincoln

Africa

American President

An interesting book I read

An interesting television program

An invention that changed the world

Ancient Egypt

Archeology

Basketball

Beach

Bill Cosby

Breakfast

Cars

Charity

Christmas

Christopher Columbus

Church

Civil war

Computers

Dance

Democracy

Dinosaur

Disney world

DNA

Dogs

Einstein

Exercise

Fashion

Halloween

Happiness

How to get good grades

Independence day

Internet

Jokes I heard

Moon

Most important person in my life

Music

My favorite movie

My favorite sports team

My favorite subject

My favorite teacher

My Friends

My mother

My School

My vacation

New inventions I would like to see

Pets

Pizza, my favorite food

Planets

Police

Prayer

Robotics

School recess

School Safety

Science and technology

Space travel

Spring break

Super bawl

Tennis

Thanksgiving

My weekend

U.S. Government

United Nations

Virginia

Welcome to America

Winter season

Notes:

_____

_____

_____

_____

_____

_____

_____

_____

_____

_____

_____

It usually takes more than three weeks to prepare a good impromptu speech.
MARK TWAIN

Example of a Great Speech

Martin Luther King, Jr. delivered the **"I Have a Dream"** speech on August 28, 1963 at the Lincoln Memorial in Washington, DC to two hundred thousand people. This speech is considered as one of the top rated speeches of all time.

The introduction and conclusion of the "I have a dream speech" are quoted below for your study. The introduction hook the audiences to the main theme of the speech and the conclusion makes the main ideas of the speech resonate in the minds of the audiences for days and months and years after the speech.

Introduction

"I am happy to join with you today in what will go down in history as the greatest demonstration for freedom in the history of our nation."

"Five score years ago, a great American, in whose symbolic shadow we stand today, signed the Emancipation Proclamation. This momentous decree came as a great beacon light of hope to millions of Negro slaves who had been seared in the flames of withering injustice...."

"But one hundred years later, the Negro still is not free. One hundred years later, the life of the Negro is still sadly crippled by the manacles of segregation and the chains of discrimination...."

Conclusion

"...Let freedom ring from Lookout Mountain of Tennessee."
"Let freedom ring from every hill and molehill of Mississippi."
"From every mountainside, let freedom ring."

 "And when this happens, when we allow freedom ring, when we let it ring from every village and every hamlet, from every state and every city, we will be able to speed up that day when all of God's children, black men and white men, Jews and Gentiles, Protestants and Catholics, will be able to join hands and sing in the words of the old Negro spiritual:"

"Free at last! Free at last!..."

Notes:

_____

_____

_____

_____

_____

_____

_____

_____

_____

_____

_____

_____

_____

A speech without a specific purpose is like a journey without a destination.
RALPH C. SMEDLEY

9

Eye Contact

Whenever you talk, either in public speaking or in less formal personal communications, it is necessary to keep good eye contact with your listeners for three important reasons.

1. Eye contact will personalize your communications. Without eye contact, your spoken words are just free sentences floating in the air. You must make your audiences feel that you are personally talking to them. Whenever you make eye contact with your audiences, they will know that you are talking to them, personally.

2. Eye contact will give you continuous feedback on how your speech is received. As you speak, you can see in the faces of your audiences the responses to your statements. Public performance is a dynamic process; it will be most effective when you can fine-tune the performance at the same time of delivering it based on the feedback you are getting. You can see the enjoyment, the excitement, the disagreement, the boredom, and all such responses in the faces of the audiences. Unless you keep good eye contact with them, you won't be able to understand the feedback of the audiences and act accordingly.

3. Eye contact will give more energy to your speech. If you do not keep good eye contact with your audiences, you may drift into a monotonous speech, one which will make you feel sluggish. It is, therefore, necessary for you, as a speaker, to feel energetic to infuse the

energy into the audiences. Hence, to keep your energy level high, you need to keep good eye contact with your audiences.

EXERCISE

1. **Prepare and perform a speech.**

2. **Make and keep good eye contact with the audiences, one at a time. Scan the audiences by turning your head from one side of the auditorium to the other and keeping good eye contact while doing this. Eye contact with each person should last for about 3-5 seconds.**

3. **If you are standing up on a podium which is not too close to the audiences to make direct person-to-person eye contact, or if the number of audiences is high, making it impossible to have personal eye contact with everybody in the audiences, consider the audiences as three or four groups, along some imaginary boundary. Make and keep eye contact with each group as you speak, keeping each eye contact for about 10 seconds.**

4. **Try to determine the audiences' emotional responses from the eye contact.**

Hand Gestures and Body Gestures

1. In every presentation, you have a visual aid, which is you, yourself. So, do not hide behind the lectern. Your whole body needs to be visible to the audience.

2. Stand straight with your feet evenly placed. Audiences are watching you, so you should do everything possible to create an excellent first impression. The way that you present yourself visually to them has a big impact on how they are going to judge you and receive your speech.

3. Hand and body gestures dramatically improve the impact of your performances. So, use your hand and body gestures to create a powerful and dramatic impact.

4. Use hand gestures as you usually use them in conversations. That way, the audiences will feel that your movements are natural.

5. Your hand and body gestures can distract the audiences, unless used carefully. So, practice the gestures well before the actual speech.

6. Do not play with your hands and fingers. Any unnecessary movements of your hands and fingers will distract your audiences.

7. Do not keep your hands behind your back or inside your pockets. You may start playing with your fingers inside your pockets, which will distract your audiences.

8. Avoid finger pointing. Usually, people do not like to be pointed at. So, instead of finger pointing, use open palm or curled finger gestures.

9. In smaller groups, gestures with one hand are better than with both hands. When the group is smaller, hand gestures using both hands can appear magnified, and hence, may cause a slight distraction, rather than adding power to your speech.

EXERCISE

1. **Prepare and perform a speech.**

2. **Practice good standing posture.**

3. **Identify areas in your speech where you can apply hand and body gestures, naturally.**

4. **Practice open palm gestures.**

5. **Practice holding your hands at your elbow level, as you deliver the speech. This will serve two purposes: (1) You will have more natural hand gestures in this position; and (2) your gestures will be more readily visible to your audiences.**

6. **Practice different styles of hand and body gestures and determine the most comfortable movements for you.**

The art of being wise is the art of knowing what to overlook.
WILLIAM JAMES

Voice Modulation - Making You Sound Better

1. Your voice is unique and you should be proud that it is. All of us sound different from each other. That is part of our personality and identity. You should be proud of your voice.

2. Use appropriate and enough pausing. Without enough pausing, your audiences may not understand your speech clearly. Pausing for speech is what white space is for a printed page – both help you to avoid the crowding of information. Moreover, your audiences will need a little time in between sentences to fully comprehend the idea or ideas that you are presenting to them. So, pause when it is appropriate; pause enough number of times; and pause for enough length of time.

3. Sound the punctuations. Sounding of punctuations is necessary to make your points clearly and emphatically to your audiences. So, make all of the punctuations audible. Use pauses and voice variations to sound the punctuations, such as periods, commas, and paragraph breaks.

4. Use context sensitive sound pitch. Whenever you have an explosive idea, sound explosive; whenever you have a sober idea, sound sober. And similarly, you should also use other context sensitive sound pitches to amplify the effect of your speech.

5. Use sound volume proportional to the number of audiences. Unless there is an electronic public address system (PA system) in the auditorium, you should adjust your sound volume proportional to the number of people there. You should be able to determine the appropriate sound volume when you begin your speech, either by sensing the responses of your audiences,

or by directly asking them whether they could hear you well and clearly.

6. Do not speak in runaway or extra long sentences. Just as it is difficult to understand runaway sentences in written communications, it is equally or more difficult to understand them in spoken communications as well. So, use shorter sentences in your speech, especially since you are a novice public speaker. As you gain more expertise in public speaking, you should be able to use longer sentences with enough pausing without causing confusion with your audiences.

7. Feel the emotions of the speech first; your voice will automatically follow the passion. Without any conscious effort, emotions do get reflected in our speaking voice. So, you should become passionate about the topic that you are speaking about and identify the emotions at various places in the speech. Once you feel the emotions of your speech, your voice will naturally reflect them.

EXERCISE

1. **Prepare a speech on a topic you are passionate or emotional about.**

2. **Identify places in the speech where you could use voice modulation.**

3. **Use a voice recorder to record your speech delivering at different speeds and with different voice modulations. Hear them back from the recorder and decide which one is the most effective one.**

4. **Perform your speech.**

Speech Practicing

1. You should prepare extremely well for the first one minute of the speech. For most public speakers, especially the novice, the first one minute of the speech is the most stressful period. Once you prepare well for that one minute, the butterflies in your stomach will be under control, and the rest of your speech will flow naturally from the first minute on. Remember, this first minute is the time for you to present the catchy introduction that you have prepared.

2. You should also prepare well for the speech conclusion. Although the conclusion time of a speech is not as stressful as the beginning, presenting a memorable conclusion creates a highly effective ending for your speech. Audiences usually remember the last part of the speech better than any other parts, and hence, you should leave them with a lasting impression of your speech through a memorable conclusion.

3. Write the main points of your speech on 3x5 cards and have them with you at the time of the speech. The fact that if you forget any points of your speech, you can easily look them up on the 3x5 cards in your hand makes you feel confident and comfortable whenever you stand up in front of the audiences.

4. Study the quotes and poems. If you have to quote a proverb or recite a poem in your speech, it is highly necessary not to make any wording mistakes with them. So, you should either study them verbatim, or read them from the 3x5 cards on which you have written them down.

5. Practice the speech in front of a mirror. By speaking in front of a mirror, you can see how your audiences will be seeing you. You will be able to catch any undesirable mannerisms or gestures that you may have by watching

yourself speak. Also, you will be able to time your speech to fit it within the allocated timeframe.

6. Practice the speech in front of your friends and family. Although this group will be small, they will be able to give you their feedback about your speech, so that you can modify and improve it.

7. Record your speech on a voice recorder. After recording it, play it back, and evaluate how you sound, whether you are giving enough pauses, whether there are any mannerisms that need to be avoided, and whether your ideas are expressed clearly and without any stuttering. Your voice on the recorder will sound slightly different from how you always hear yourself; this is natural, so do not be bothered by it.

8. Record your speech using a video camera. After recording it, play it back, and evaluate your presentation style, your standing posture, and your body and hand gestures. Pay special attention to catch any undesirable body movements and playing with your fingers.

EXERCISE

1. **Prepare a speech that includes some quotes or poems.**

2. **Use 3x5 cards to write down the main points of your speech.**

3. **Prepare a catchy introduction and a memorable conclusion.**

4. **Study the first minute of your speech well.**

5. **Study the voice modulation and sounding of punctuations for the quotes or poems.**

6. **Practice your speech in front of a mirror.**

7. **Practice your speech in front of your family or friends.**

8. **Use a voice recorder to record your speech and evaluate it.**

9. **Use a video camera to record your speech and evaluate it.**

10. **Perform your speech.**

Professionalism

You should appear and act professionally during your speech.

1. Dress appropriately. Whenever you stand in front of the audiences dressed appropriately, your formal appearance will give you more credibility than you will get, otherwise.

2. Be neat and conduct yourself accordingly. The neatness in your appearance and conduct will positively influence the audiences' heart before you even begin your speech.

3. Understand what is expected of you. Before you begin your speech, you should understand clearly what is expected of you. Otherwise, your presentation will not satisfy the needs of the audiences. If you don't satisfy the needs of the audiences, even if your speech is wonderful otherwise, it will be a failure.

4. Be serious. If you are not serious, your audiences will not be either. If your audiences are not serious, they won't pay you the attention or give you the respect that you need for a successful presentation.

5. Be confident. Audiences love a speaker who is confident, and so, you should prepare yourself until you are confident. If you are confident about your knowledge of the speech material, and your ability to do an excellent job of public speaking, your confidence will also be observable to the audiences.

6. Be prepared. For any job, public speaking or anything else, you need to be prepared. Preparation will bring in confidence.

EXERCISE

1. Dress professionally whenever you have a formal presentation.

2. Ask some questions, such as the ones below, to understand what is expected of you:

   a.   Who are the audiences?

   b.   How long are you expected to speak to the audiences?

   c.   How long is the overall meeting itself?

   d.   Are you speaking at the beginning, the middle, or at the end of the meeting?

   e.   Who are the other speakers?

   f.   Why is this speech topic important?

3. Perform your speech.

Notes: _____

_____

_____

_____

_____

_____

_____

_____

_____

_____

Emergency Management

There will be situations when you lose your train of thought, or simply forget the next point in your speech. Use any of the techniques that follow to handle such situations.

When you forget - DO:

1. Pause. This will give you the time with which to recall your train of thought.

2. Refer to your notes. But, do not take too much time trying to refer to your notes because your audiences are waiting for you to continue.

3. Repeat the last idea with an emphasis. "Let me repeat…" This will reinforce the idea in the minds of your audiences and give you traction to start your train of thought again.

4. Use a filler story. This will ease your tension and make your audiences more relaxed.

5. Ask for questions from the audiences. This will give you time to pause and put your audiences in a participatory mode. Most of the time, this technique will bring back your train of thought.

When you forget – DON'T:

1. Do not ramble on. It will make it obvious to the audiences that either you forgot the next point or you do not have any more points to talk about, but do not know how to conclude.

2. Do not look elsewhere. Taking your eye contact off of the audiences and looking at the ceiling or floor makes it too obvious to your audiences that you lost the continuity of your speech.

3. Do not stutter or keep on repeating the same sentences and words.

4. Do not be frightened. Forgetting a point is not the end of the world.

EXERCISE

1. **Study a few filler stories and jokes that you can use in different speeches.**

2. **Practice telling filler stories or jokes during the speech.**

3. **Practice asking questions during the speech.**

4. **Perform the speech.**

Meeting Administration

1. You should understand all the housekeeping rules because you need to explain these rules to the audiences.

2. You should understand that the smooth running of the meeting is your responsibility. So, you should pay attention to each part of the meeting and its overall flow.

3. When giving instructions, make sure that the audiences understand them well. Then observe how the audiences are following through with your instructions and provide them positive and corrective feedback.

4. Be fair to all participants and audiences when making decisions.

EXERCISE

1. **Perform as the Master of Ceremony of a meeting.**

   ■ **Make sure that you give a good introduction to the speaker**

   ■ **Also, after the presentation by the speaker, give a few postive comments on the presentation.**

2. **Perform your speech.**

Notes:

_____

_____

_____

_____

_____

_____

_____

_____

_____

_____

_____

_____

_____

_____

_____

_____

_____

_____

_____

_____

Giving Instructions to Others

Giving clear and concise instructions to make people do a task is one of the most important skills that a leader should have. Giving instructions and leading a task require three areas of skills: Leadership skills, Communication skills, and Interpersonal skills.

1. Your announcements and instructions should be simple enough to understand. There are people with different comprehension levels in your audiences. So, your instructions should be simple enough for all of them to comprehend or understand.

2. Explain the instructions in a sequential pattern. The instructions should follow a 1-2-3 pattern, so that people can follow them without any confusion.

3. A picture is worth a thousand words. If you can draw a picture or show a demonstration of what you are explaining, your audiences will understand it more clearly.

4. After the instructions, check the understanding of the audiences. Since you want the audiences to act according to your instructions, it is necessary to make sure that they understood your instructions correctly. So, review their understanding before letting them start their actions.

EXERCISE

1. Select a game that can be played by a group of people.

2. Exercise your leadership skills by:

   - Selecting the participants.

   - Coordinating their activities.

   - Managing time restrictions.

   - Managing the noise level.

   - Managing the order.

3. Exercise your communication skills by:

   - Explaining the rules clearly - maybe, with some key examples.

4. Exercise your interpersonal skills by:

   - Keeping the game as a fun event.

   - Managing the participants firmly, but in a friendly manner.

Talking and eloquence are not the same: to speak, and to speak well are two things. A fool may talk, but a wise man speaks.

BEN JOHNSON

Young Speakers Club
Course Register and Performance Record

Student Name: _____

Level: _____

Date	Program	Title	Points	Certified By

10/8

RICE PUBLIC LIBRARY
8 WENTWORTH ST.
KITTERY, MAINE 03904
207-439-1553